A DESK BOOK OF
PLAIN ENGLISH

By A. W. ROWE

Headmaster David Lister High School
Kingston upon Hull

Assisted by J. B. L. ALLEN
Headmaster Misbourne Secondary School
Buckinghamshire

Illustrated by HARO

D1580232

BASIL BLACKWELL · OXFORD

CONTENTS

		PAGE
To the Teacher		iii
To the Student: How to Use this Reference Book .		iv

PART I: RULES FOR USING PUNCTUATION MARKS

1.	Full Stop	1, 2
2.	Comma	3, 4
3.	Semicolon	5, 6
4.	Colon	7
5.	Brackets	8
6.	Dashes	8, 9
7.	Quotation Marks	9, 10
8.	Question Mark	11
9.	Exclamation Mark	11

PART II: RULES FOR USING WORDS

10.	Nouns	12–14
11.	Pronouns	14–16
12.	Verbs	17–23
13.	Adjectives	24, 25
14.	Adverbs	26–28
15.	Prepositions	29–32
16.	Troublesome Words	32–34
17.	Capital Letters	35, 36
18.	Apostrophes	36–38
19.	Indefinite Article	39
20.	Hyphens	40

PART III: RULES FOR MAKING AND USING SENTENCES

21.	Singular or Plural Verb?	41–43
22.	Tense (or Time)	44–50
23.	Position of Words	51, 52
24.	Negatives	52–54
25.	Paragraphs	55
	Index	56–60

© *Basil Blackwell & Mott, Ltd., 1965*

Reprinted 1967, 1971, 1972

ISBN 0 631 95990 4

PRINTED IN GREAT BRITAIN
FOR BASIL BLACKWELL & MOTT LTD.
BY COMPTON PRINTING LTD., LONDON AND AYLESBURY
AND BOUND BY
THE KEMP HALL BINDERY, OXFORD

TO THE TEACHER

THIS pocket reference book provides the pupil with an essential tool for improving his English, and one which up to now has been lacking.

Its contents are based upon research into what are the commonest errors made in written English in secondary schools. It will be as useful to slower first-year groups as to older students working for examinations.

The teacher need only *indicate* the mistake, using whatever method he wishes.

For instance, suppose that "to" is written instead of "too," or "was" instead of "were." The teacher crosses the word out and this is the signal to the pupil to look it up in the *Index*. That in turn directs him to the page where examples of the correct usage are laid out and so he is himself able to put his own mistake right. Again, if a punctuation mistake has been made, the teacher can use his own sign to send the student either to the *Index* or direct to *Part I: Rules for Using Punctuation Marks* which, because it has been concentrated into only 11 pages, can be used by the student quickly to diagnose and correct his error.

Pupils will work at different levels. The less able will *imitate* what is correct and this, after all, is how most people acquire the greater part of their command of their own language. The abler will add *understanding* to imitation.

The teacher should at the start make sure that the pupil thoroughly understands and can use the very simple *Index*, for this is the key to the success of the book. Spelling errors are deliberately not dealt with; it is assumed that everyone will have his own dictionary.

TO THE STUDENT

WHATEVER school subjects you are at present studying, you must use English to study them successfully. No matter what job you do when you leave school, or how you spend your spare time, you will be using English.

This is a pocket reference book to help you to write correct English. Keep your own copy by your side whenever you are writing.

You will often hear it said that we learn by making mistakes. This is true, but only partly true. We learn nothing when we go on making the same mistake over and over again. *To learn from our mistakes we must understand why they were wrong and how to put them right; then we must put them right and take care not to make the same mistakes again.*

This book will enable you to do this. The key to its successful use is the *Index*. Make sure at once that you understand how to use it.

Even professional writers have similar reference books by their side as they write, so that they can look up points about which they are doubtful. In this way they check that what they are about to write is in fact correct. Note that you can use this book in exactly the same way—you can check that what you are going to write is in fact correct *before* you write it.

Writing is a craft, just as metalwork or needlework is, and you cannot be a good craftsman until you know how to use your tools and materials correctly. This book is your craftsman's manual. It will help you to become skilled in the craft of writing.

PART ONE

RULES FOR USING PUNCTUATION MARKS

THE job of punctuation is to help to make your meaning clear beyond doubt. This is why it is just as important as spelling. Although there are different ways of punctuating, until you are an experienced writer it is safer to follow a few simple rules. For instance, always read through your own work and listen to the sense of it. Where the sense demands a pause, *there* you must have a punctuation mark.

The following examples of correct punctuation are here to guide you. Study them. See how far the books you are reading follow these rules. Discuss points of difference with your teacher. Refer to this section when you are in doubt about punctuating.

1. FULL STOP

A FULL STOP ENDS A SENTENCE.

It tells you where the sense comes to a "full stop."

1. He smiles •

2. John sees the man •

3. John Smith noticed the man as he came through the hedge •

4. "I will come with you," John said •

5. You called me, I came, and we went on together.

6. We stopped suddenly. "There he is," I said, "over there, look." I pointed to the tall man, who was pausing uncertainly on the edge of the pavement, a white walking-stick clenched in his right hand and the missing parcel hugged to his chest.

FULL STOPS MARK ABBREVIATIONS

e.g. = for example
a.m. = before noon
N.B. = take particular note of this
R.S.V.P. = please reply
A.D. = (year) since Christ
etc. (*et cetera*) = and so on
Rt. Hon. = Right Honourable
i.e. = that is
p.m. = afternoon
P.T.O. = please turn over
B.C. = (year) before Christ
Rev. = Reverend
M.P. = Member of Parliament

FULL STOPS ARE PUT AFTER THE INITIALS OF A PERSON'S NAME

1. He is P. H. E. W. Brown.
2. Miss J. V. Smith sat quite still.

2. COMMA

Commas mark where the short pauses come, and so help to make the sense clear.

COMMAS SEPARATE THE ITEMS IN A LIST.

1. His pockets contained string, toffee-papers, a marble, two penknives, a piece of chalk, several small pieces of blotting paper, a bent drawing pin, a pet mouse, the core of an apple, and a dog-eared and dirty piece of paper containing what looked like signatures written in blood.

2. Mr. White can still move easily, quickly, vigorously, and skilfully.

3. You can come to-morrow, on Friday, next week, or any other time that suits you.

4. He is David Davies, Esq., M.C., M.A., of 101 Stanford Place, London, S.W.1.

COMMAS ARE NEEDED TO SEPARATE THE DIFFERENT PARTS OF A SENTENCE. THE PARTS MAY BE ONE WORD, OR GROUPS OF WORDS.

1. Further, smoking is not allowed.
   (*Compare:* Further smoking is not allowed.)
2. Shortly after, she had passed her examination.
   (*Compare:* Shortly after she had passed her examination, she left school.)
3. The reason is, no one saw him.
4. For fear Alfred should miss his train, his father took him to the station an hour too soon.
5. In order not to let the team down, all three of us trained harder than ever before.
6. Miss Pusey was, alas, no longer alive.

7. I sent for you, if you really want to know, to ask you to help me out of a difficulty.

8. "It won't work," Donald said, "try it this way, and then it's bound to work."

COMMAS HELP TO SEPARATE THE OPENING AND CLOSING OF A LETTER FROM ITS CONTENTS.

1. Dear Ted,
   Something wonderful ....
   ....
                    Yours sincerely,
                             Francis

2. My dear Jane,
   Your news came as ....
   ....
                    Affectionately yours,
                             Freda

3. Sir,
   Your letter of 21 February ....
   ....
                    Yours faithfully,
                             B. G. Marston

COMMAS WITH ADDRESSES.

On envelopes:

1.   J. W. WATSON, Esq., O.B.E., M.Ed.,
            April Cottage,
            Bunkers Hill,
            ST. IVES,
            Cornwall

At the beginning of letters:

2.   27 Payne Street,
               London, S.W.1

3. SEMICOLON

A semicolon marks a pause longer than that marked by a comma.

SEMICOLONS SEPARATE COMPLICATED ITEMS IN A LIST.

1. His study contained a dozen or more bookcases, each seven feet high and crammed tight with books; a big table piled high with files, loose papers, books, rulers, pens, pencils, ink, and a glass jar full of paper-clips; two huge and very ancient easy-chairs, with more books and papers in confused heaps on the seats and arms; a carpet snowed under with even more papers and books and files.

2. The little guide's hat, several sizes too large for her, was balanced precariously on her ears; her water-bottle, big as a bucket, hung down to her knees; from a large bag stuffed to the brim, her raincoat cascaded to the ground and dragged in the mud at each weary step.

SEMICOLONS SEPARATE IDEAS OF EQUAL IMPORTANCE WHICH ARE PUT IN CONTRAST WITH EACH OTHER.

1. The boys are quiet; the girls are noisy.

2. Speech is silver; silence is golden.

3. The girls in this school are good at English and weak in mathematics; the boys are good at mathematics and weak in English.

Note that you could replace the semicolons by full stops, but the effect would be jerky, and the sense of contrast would be less.

SEMICOLONS SEPARATE LONGER PARTS OF A SENTENCE, ESPECIALLY WHEN THESE ARE THEMSELVES SUBDIVIDED BY COMMAS.

1. She will let you see your friend, if the doctor will agree; but, if he forbids it, you will have to wait till the next day.

2. John is a good friend, who will never let you down; for example, however much he was tempted, he would never betray your secrets.

3. "Pop" singers, especially those with long hair, are much liked by some; others find them very tiresome.

4. COLON

1. These are the chief exports of Australia: wheat, wool, butter, cheese, mutton.

2. It was a most fortunate find: a case of nuts, two kegs of water, one unfortunately broken and half-empty; a side of salt beef; and half-a-dozen tins of biscuits.

3. Here are the most important points: one, keep hidden; two, don't make a sound; three, stay on watch until I relieve you.

A COLON IS OFTEN USED INSTEAD OF A COMMA TO INTRODUCE A QUOTATION OR A TITLE.

1. The quotation which you were looking for goes like this: "Stone walls do not a prison make, nor iron bars a cage."

2. Read Section B: "Words and How to Use Them."

3. The picture is a fine one: "The White Horse," by Paul Gauguin.

7

5. BRACKETS

BRACKETS ENCLOSE WORDS WHICH GIVE ADDITIONAL EXPLANATION OR INFORMATION.

1. The directions for putting the television set together are important (see page 3 of the manual).

2. The bus timetable shows that the Sunday services (Schedule B) are few.

3. Do Question 1 and two others. (Marks will be deducted for poor spelling.)

6. DASHES

A SINGLE DASH MARKS A SHARP BREAK IN THE SENTENCE.

1. Power, money, possession, friends — all were lost.

2. You may do it — at your own risk.

3. Mary may come too, if she wants to — and I think she will come.

DASHES CAN BE USED INSTEAD OF BRACKETS TO ENCLOSE WORDS WHICH GIVE ADDITIONAL INFORMATION.

1. Philip James — a blackguard if ever there was one — is coming here to-night.

2. If he succeeds — and who dare say that he will not? — he will be the first man ever to do it.

Note that dashes give rather more emphasis than brackets to the words between them.

7. QUOTATION MARKS

QUOTATION MARKS ENCLOSE THE ACTUAL WORDS OF THE SPEAKER.

1. George said, "Come here."

"No, I won't," Mary replied.

"Come here at once," he went on. "If you don't, I shall make you."

Note that you normally begin a new line each time for a different speaker.

QUOTATION MARKS ARE NEEDED WHENEVER YOU SET DOWN WORDS WRITTEN BY ANOTHER PERSON. *The actual words are "Quotations."*

1. The commandment reads, "Thou shalt not kill."

2. The story begins: "I was born in the Cornish village of Carbis Bay."

QUOTATION MARKS ARE USED WHEN WRITING TITLES OF BOOKS, PAINTINGS, ETC.

1. **"The Road to Fame"** is a good book.

2. We like the art master's new painting, **"Rockets,"** very much.

3. The house is called **"The Elms."**

QUOTATION MARKS ENCLOSE FOREIGN WORDS AND PHRASES WHEN WRITING.

1. The French phrase, **"à la campagne,"** means **"in the open air."**

2. **"In vino veritas"** is a true saying.

QUOTATION MARKS ARE NEEDED FOR SLANG EXPRESSIONS.

1. They were so tired that they **"hit the hay"** at once.

2. He never **"uses his loaf,"** poor lad.

3. She told Susan that she didn't **"dig"** that at all.

8. QUESTION MARK

A QUESTION MARK ENDS A DIRECT QUESTION.

1. "Why?" he asked.
2. What will happen next?
3. "Are you coming, Tom?" Sam shouted.

9. EXCLAMATION MARK

AN EXCLAMATION MARK IS USED FOR EMPHASIS.

1. "Oh!" she cried.
2. "Ah! that's all very well," he said.
3. "How annoying!" Christopher said.
4. What a pity!

HARO

11

PART TWO

RULES FOR USING WORDS

WE all make some mistakes when we use words. The following rules will help you to correct the commonest mistakes you may make. Refer to them also when you are in difficulty.

Imitate and learn from the examples of words used correctly and so gradually avoid making the same mistakes over and over again. Be sure that you understand the examples: if not, discuss them with your teacher. When you understand the reason behind a particular usage, you will have gone a long way towards remembering it.

10. NOUNS

A NOUN IS THE WORD WE USE TO REFER TO A PERSON, ANIMAL, PLACE, OR THING.

1. He is a **man**.
2. It was only a **dog** howling.
3. The **town** was very quiet.
4. **Litter** covered the **pavement**.

A PROPER NOUN IS THE NAME WE GIVE TO A PARTICULAR PERSON, ANIMAL, PLACE, OR THING, AND BEGINS WITH A CAPITAL LETTER.

1. This man is called **Brown**.
2. **England** is where I live.
3. **London** stands on the **River Thames**.
4. Thirty days hath **September**, **April**, **June**, and **November**.
5. **Tuesday**, **Wednesday**, and **Thursday** are my three favourite days at school.

2. My cat, **"Jacko,"** has a tail 26 inches long.

7. The book I have been reading is called **"Warrior Scarlet."**

8. **"Firefly"** is the fastest little sailing boat of them all.

NOUNS CAN BE EITHER SINGULAR (*man*, *dog*, *house*) OR PLURAL (*men*, *dogs*, *houses*). HERE ARE SOME RULES FOR WRITING PLURALS CORRECTLY.

1. *Most nouns add* **s**: boy boy**s**; chimney chimney**s**; donkey donkey**s**; game game**s**; girl girl**s**; herd herd**s**.

2. *Nouns ending in -x, -s, -sh, -ss, -ch, add* **es**: box box**es**; brush brush**es**; church church**es**; gas gas**es**; glass glass**es**; match match**es**; mess mess**es**; porch porch**es**; process process**es**.

3. *These important nouns in -o add* **es**: cargo cargo**es**; echo echo**es**; hero hero**es**; negro negro**es**; potato potato**es**; tomato tomato**es**; volcano volcano**es**.

Some common exceptions: cameo cameo**s**; cuckoo cuckoo**s**; curio curio**s**; magneto magneto**s**; piano piano**s**; portfolio portfolio**s**; radio radio**s**; solo solo**s**.

4. *Most nouns ending in -f and -fe CHANGE -f- to -v- and ADD* es: calf cal**ves**; half hal**ves**; knife kni**ves**; leaf lea**ves**; life li**ves**; loaf loa**ves**; self sel**ves**; sheaf shea**ves**; shelf shel**ves**; thief thie**ves**; wife wi**ves**; wolf wol**ves**.

Note: hoof hoof**s** or hoo**ves**; proof proof**s**; roof roof**s**; safe safe**s**; scarf scarf**s** or scar**ves**; wharf wharf**s** or whar**ves**.

5. *Some nouns that end in -y CHANGE the -y to* **-ies**: army arm**ies**; baby bab**ies**; city cit**ies**; lady lad**ies**; lorry lorr**ies**; penny penn**ies** (or pence).

This happens when the letter before the -y is NOT -a-, -e-, -i-, -o-, -u-.

6. *A few nouns CHANGE the VOWEL:* foot f**ee**t; goose g**ee**se; man m**e**n; tooth t**ee**th; woman wom**e**n.

7. *A few nouns have -en plurals:* child child**ren**; ox ox**en**.

8. *Some nouns REMAIN the SAME:* cod cod; deer deer; fowl fowl; gallows gallows; grouse grouse; haddock haddock; hake hake; halibut halibut; herring herring; mackerel mackerel; moose moose; salmon salmon; sheep sheep; wildfowl wildfowl.

11. PRONOUNS

PRONOUNS STAND IN PLACE OF NOUNS.

1. **He** [= John Maine] is very heavy.
2. **She** [= the "Queen Mary"] is two days out from Southampton.
3. **It** [= Birmingham] is a big city.
4. **They** [= the cars] were travelling at 90 miles an hour.

"I" OR "ME"?

1. Lucy and **I** went.
Test by saying aloud: "Lucy went"; "*I* went"; "*me* went."
"Me went" sounds absurd. Therefore "I" is obviously right.

2. He gave it to Lucy and **me**.
Test by saying aloud: "He gave it to Lucy"; "He gave it to **me**"; *"He gave it to* **I**." *"To I" sounds absurd. Therefore "to me" is right.*

3. He and **I** will do it.
*Test by saying "He will do it"; "***I***" will do it. Obviously not "***Me*** will do it."*

4. Your father said he would come for you and **me** at seven o'clock.

Test by saying "He would come for you"; "He would come for **me**." *"He would come for I" is obviously wrong.*

Note also this common phrase: Between you and *me*.

"HE" OR "HIM"? "SHE" OR "HER"?

When in doubt, use the same test.

1. Jack and **he** went.
"*Jack went*"; "*he went*." *Obviously not "***Him*** went."*
2. Judith and **she** will do it.
"*Judith will do it*"; "**She** *will do it*."
3. **He** gave it to Jack and **him**.
"*He gave it to Jack*"; "*He gave it to* **him**."
4. **He** gave it to Lucy and **her**.
5. **He** and **she** are the only ones to volunteer
6. "Your father said he would come for **him** and **her** at seven o'clock, but the others can go earlier."

AFTER "AS" AND "THAN," WHICH PRONOUN DO I WRITE?
"I" OR "ME"? "HE" OR "HIM"? "SHE" OR "HER"?

1. Bill is as old as **I** (= I am.)
2. His sister is taller than **he** (= he is.)
3. Luck favoured you more than **her** (= than it favoured her.)
4. It made more difference to you than to **me** (= than it did to me.)

"WHO" OR "WHOM"?

1. **Who** saw the boy?
2. **Who** is going with her?
3. *With* **whom** is she going?
4. It was Mr. Green **who** sang in the street.
5. Miss Jones, **who** owns the cats, is a very kind woman.
6. Miss Smith, *to* **whom** the dogs belong, was angry.

"HERS," "OURS," "YOURS," "THEIRS," SHOW POSSESSION WITHOUT AN APOSTROPHE.

1. The red ball is **hers** (= her *ball*.)
2. Your buns are over there; **ours** are on the tray (= our *buns*.)
3. I end letters to friends with "**Yours** sincerely" (= your sincere *friend*.)
4. Our budgerigar is green, **theirs** is blue.
5. "Yes, **ours** is green, but **theirs** is pale blue."

DO NOT WRITE "THEM" WHEN YOU MEAN "THESE" OR "THOSE."

1. **These** are his (= these books, NOT *them* books).
2. **Those** are the ones who stole the apples (= *those* boys, NOT *them* boys).

12. VERBS

1. He **eats** good food.

2. They **are fighting.**

3. He **is being** funny.
4. She **lives** in Canada.
5. Tom **was becoming**
lazy.

6. That plant **grows** an inch a week.

TROUBLESOME VERBS WHICH ARE OFTEN USED AND SPELT
WRONGLY.

1. BEAR (= *carry or endure.*)
   (*a*) We should **bear** one another's burdens.
   (*b*) I **bore** him on my back.
   (*c*) He **bore** the pain bravely.
   (*d*) She was **borne** away on a stretcher.
   Note: The plane was *airborne* at once.

2. BEAR (children.)
   (*a*) It is very sad; she has never been able to **bear a**
   child.
   (*b*) She **bore** a child.
   (*c*) He was **born** on 1st July, 1915.
   (*d*) A son was **born** to her on Friday.
   (*e*) She has **borne** three daughters.

17

3. BEAT (*You beat the other competitor.*)

        beat
(*a*) I ~~won~~ Julia at table-tennis.

              beat
(*b*) Our team ~~won~~ theirs.

             beat
(*c*) Tom's pony ~~won~~ Mary's.

        beat
(*d*) Did she ~~win~~ her?

4. BORROW (*You borrow something FROM someone*).

            borrow
(*a*) "Please may I ~~lend~~ a racket from you?"

            borrow
(*b*) "We've come to ~~lend~~ the football."

5. CHOOSE.

    (*a*) He **chooses** the black one this time.
    (*b*) **Choose** what you want at once.
    (*c*) **Choosing** a new dress is fun.
    (*d*) He will have to **choose** now; his sister will be **choosing** later.
    (*e*) We **chose** the car yesterday.
    (*f*) Once you **have chosen** it, you must stick to your choice.

6. HAVE.

        have
(*a*) She could ~~of~~ sung it.

have
(b) She could not ~~of~~ sung it.

have
(c) "We couldn't ~~of~~ sung it," John said.

have
(d) They might ~~of~~ played.

have
(e) "He mightn't ~~of~~ done it," said Freda.

have
(f) Jim must ~~of~~ gone.

have
(g) Mary said, "They mustn't ~~of~~ gone yet."

have
(h) He ought to ~~of~~ played.

have
(i) Father said, "She oughtn't to ~~of~~ done it."
(*NOT* "She didn't ought to have done it.")

7. LAY.

(a) She **lays** the table neatly and quickly.
(b) **Lay** the baby in the cradle.

19

(*c*) The hen **laid** an enormous egg.

(*d*) We have **laid** our plans.

(*e*) He **had laid** the carpet before she came home.

(*f*) He used to **lay** bets, then he wisely gave it up, but now he **is laying** bets again.

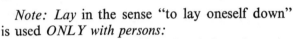

(*g*) They **laid** him on the operating table.

> *Note:* Lay in the sense "to lay oneself down" is used *ONLY with persons:*
> i. She *lays herself* on the sand and closes her eyes.
> ii. *Lay yourself* down and rest a little.
> iii. The girl *laid herself* on the bed and began to cry.
> iv. They *have laid themselves* flat.

8. LET (= *allow; permit*).
   (*a*) "**Let's** eat it" (= "Let us").
   (*b*) **Let** him go.
   (*c*) His mother will not **let** him play football in the street.
   (*d*) I shall **let** him see the cat.

9. LET LOOSE.
   (*a*) He **lets** the greyhound **loose** and it shoots away.
   (*b*) She **let loose** the captive birds, one by one.
   (*c*) "Why have you **let loose** all the captive animals?"
   (*d*) Stan is **letting** the pigeon loose, and Sylvia is about to **let loose** the dove.

10. LIE (*down*).

(*a*) She **lies** on the sand and closes her eyes.

(*b*) **Lie** down and rest a little.

(*c*) The girl **lay** on the bed and began to cry.

(*d*) He **has lain** there now for two hours without moving.

(*e*) If the convict **had lain** still, he would not have been noticed.

(*f*) She has gone **to lie** down.

(*g*) "You always used to **lie** down at this hour," he said, "and you **are lying** down now."

11. LOSE.

(*a*) He **loses** his only chance.

(*b*) **Lose** it and I will beat you.

(*c*) She **is losing** her temper.

(*d*) He **lost** his very first pay-packet on his way home.

(*e*) Everything was **lost**.

(*f*) It is satisfying to win, but you must not mind if you **lose**.

12. OUGHT.

ought not
(*a*) He ~~didn't ought~~ to go to the races so often.

ought not
(*b*) He ~~hadn't ought~~ to have come here without asking permission.

13. TEACH.

teach
(*a*) I will ~~learn~~ you to swim.

taught
(*b*) Robert has ~~learnt~~ his dog many tricks.

taught
(*c*) Elizabeth is being ~~learnt~~ French.

(*d*) The bears have
taught
been ~~learnt~~ to dance.

14. USED NOT TO.

used not
(*a*) He ~~usen't~~ to be so unkind to his brother.

Note: Some people would accept "usen't", especially in the North Country, but it is probably clearer not to use it.

15. WAKE, *or* WAKE UP.

    (*a*) I **wake** each morning at seven.

    (*b*) She **woke up** yesterday at six.

    (*c*) **Wakened** by the alarm, he sat up.

    (*d*) **Waking up** each morning at five, he never went to sleep again.

16. TO HAVE GONE.

    gone
She has ~~went~~ down the road to buy some shoes.

WHEREVER POSSIBLE, USE A MORE PRECISE, MORE MEANING-FUL VERB THAN "GOT."

    received
1. I ~~got~~ your letter.

    caught
2. He ~~got~~ a cold.

    won
3. She ~~got~~ first prize.

    was
4. The hen ~~got~~ run over.

Note: "At least I have **got** what he wanted" *is acceptable usage.*

13. ADJECTIVES

AN ADJECTIVE DESCRIBES A NOUN OR PRONOUN.

1. John is a **fat** boy.

2. The **black** rat disappeared.

3. She was **old** and **wrinkled**.

WHEN YOU COMPARE ONLY TWO THINGS, USE "-ER" OR "MORE."

taller
1. Mary is the ~~tallest~~ of the two.

older
2. "Who is ~~oldest~~, Sam or Jack?"

more
3. Which kitten is the ~~most~~ active of the pair?

4. That collection of coins is fascinating, but this **one**

more
is ~~most~~ fascinating.

TROUBLESOME ADJECTIVES OFTEN USED AND SPELT
WRONGLY.

1. ITS.
   (a) The dog is chewing **its** bone. (Whose bone? *Its* bone.)
   (b) "The teapot is getting cold, Mother. Where is **its** cosy?" (Which cosy? *Its* cosy.)
   (c) "It's very annoying. Here's the box, but where on earth is **its** cover?"
   Note: "It's" *always stands for* "It is."

2. QUIET.
   (a) The dog is **quiet**; he is lying asleep in his basket.
   (b) It was **quiet** outside; all noise of traffic had ceased.
   (c) "**Quiet!** The examination has begun."

3. THEIR.
   (a) The family quarrelled over **their** evening meal. (Whose meal? *Their* meal.)
   (b) All the chisels have had **their** edges ruined. (Which edges? **Their** edges.)
   (c) "There is the place where **their** footprints were found!"

4. WHOSE.

   Whose
   (a) Who's ball is that?

   whose
   (b) He does not know who's pen it is.

   whose
   (c) "Who's going to tell me who's little girl she is?"
   Note: "Who's" *always stands for* "Who is."

14. ADVERBS

THE WORDS IN BOLD PRINT ARE ADVERBS.

1. He sang **loudly**.
2. She was **extraordinarily**
   slow.

3. Mary landed **heavily** on
   her face.

4. **Thoughtfully** he studied the page.
5. I never thought you would act so **unkindly**.

REMEMBER THE "-LY" ENDING OF ADVERBS WHEN YOU USE
THEM TO ADD TO THE MEANING OF THE VERB.

       slowly.
1. He spoke slow.

       sadly.
2. Doris went home sad.

       heavily.
3. It was raining heavy.

       disastrously.
4. The concert turned out disastrous.

       quickly.
5. They ran away, so he said, very quick.

  Quietly   **carefully**
6. Quiet and careful they moved forward.

1. OFF.

(a) Donald went **off** ~~of~~ in a huff.

(b) The hikers set **off** ~~of~~ wearily once more.

(c) Sheila stepped **off** ~~of~~ the pavement and nearly got run over.

(d) "Break the branch **off** ~~of~~ and bring it here."

(e) The dance is **off** ~~of~~, the band cannot come.

(f) Diane jumped feet first **off** ~~of~~ the spring-board.

(g) "Come **off** ~~of~~ it," he said, "you can't fool me."

2. QUITE.

   (*a*) It was **quite** an occasion when my big sister got married.

   (*b*) Walter went **quite** white: there was hardly any colour in his face.

   (*c*) "Keep **quite** still, there's a wasp on your neck."

   (*d*) He had **quite** enough after working for twelve hours without stopping.

3. THERE.

   There

   (*a*) ~~Their~~ is the place where I lost it.

   there

   (*b*) "The necklace is over ~~their~~ in the grass, I can see it shining."

   there,

   (*c*) Their friends were all ~~their~~, packed together in one corner.

4. WHERE.

   "Where

   (*a*) "~~Were~~ have I put my umbrella?" Mary said.

   where

   (*b*) They did not know ~~were~~ to go next.

   where

   (*c*) They did not know ~~were~~ their hats and coats were.

15. PREPOSITIONS

A PREPOSITION SUGGESTS RELATIONSHIP.

1. The cow **in** the field gazed **at** the man **on** the horse.
2. She went **into** the playground early **in** the afternoon.

SOMETIMES THE PREPOSITION TO BE USED VARIES WITH THE SENSE. LEARN AND IMITATE THESE.

1. AGREE WITH (*a person, a statement already made, an action already performed*).
   - (*a*) "I *agree* **with** *you*, you're quite right, it's in the dictionary."
   - (*b*) "Father *agrees* **with** what you did."

2. AGREE ON (a matter).
   - (*a*) "Let us *agree* **on** what we will do next."
   - (*b*) John and Harry cannot *agree* **on** the time they will leave.
   - (*c*) "Please stop quarrelling and do try to *agree* **on** the date of the next meeting."

3. AGREE TO (*something in the future*).
   - (*a*) Susan will not *agree* **to** your coming to her party.
   - (*b*) "All right, then, let's *agree* **to** differ."
   - (*c*) "Will you *agree* **to** my proposition?"

4. COMPARE WITH (*to note the resemblances and differences*).
   - (*a*) *Compared* **with** her sister, Helen is no beauty.
   - (*b*) John is so pleasant *compared* **with** Bill, who has such a bad temper.
   - (*c*) As watch-dogs, Airedales cannot be *compared* **with** Alsatians.
   - (*d*) They *compared* the blue boat **with** the white.

29

5. CONFIDE IN (*someone*).

   (*a*) I will *confide* **in** you, but you must promise to keep my secret.

   (*b*) It was a mistake to *confide* **in** her; she only betrayed your trust.

6. CONFIDE (*something*) TO (*someone*).

   (*a*) Jack *confided* the story of the theft **to** Monica.

   (*b*) Dr. James mistakenly *confided* the secret formula **to** the spy.

7. CONSIST OF (*material things*).

   (*a*) The cake *consisted* **of** flour, fat, eggs, sugar, and sultanas.

   (*b*) The security precautions *consist* **of** nothing but a padlock and chain on the main gate.

8. DIFFER FROM (*to be different, to disagree with*).

   (*a*) This box *differs* **from** that one—for one thing, it is so much bigger.

   (*b*) They *differ* **from** each other in many respects.

   (*c*) I *differ* **from** you over how to interpret the rules.

9. DIFFERENT FROM.

   (*a*) This pencil is *different* **from** that one because it is thicker.

   (*b*) She told you a *different* story **from** the one she told me.

10. PREFER *is followed by* TO *or* RATHER THAN.

    (*a*) She *prefers* brown sugar **to** white.

    (*b*) Of course I *preferred* going home **to** staying there.

    (*c*) She *preferred* to sit **rather than** to stand.

    (*d*) He *prefers* to play tennis **rather than** watch.

11. TIRED OF (*somebody or something = fed up with*).
    (*a*) Dr. Johnson said that those people who were *tired of* London were *tired* **of** life.

(*b*) "I'm *tired* to death **of** stew every day!"

12. TIRED BY *or* WITH (*tired out*).

    (*a*) *Tired* out **by** his exertions, he fell asleep.
    (*b*) No wonder he is *tired* **with** all that digging.
    (*c*) No wonder he is *tired* **by** all that digging.
    (*d*) She was utterly *tired* out **by** her children.

USEFUL WORDS WITH THEIR PREPOSITIONS.

1. Would you care to *comment* **on** his work? (= Would you care to say something about his work?)

2. You are not to *communicate* **with** them. (= You are not to get in touch with them.)

3. We must now *confer* **with** our partners to find out what they think about it. (= We must now have a talk with our partners . . . .)

4. You should not have *connived* **at** his deceit. (= You should not have helped him to deceive.)

5. Phyllis was very *conscious* **of** her appearance. (= Phyllis was very particular about her appearance.)

6. *Contrast* his behaviour **with** hers.

7. What can we *deduce* **from** all the clues? (What can we conclude from all the clues?)

8. The old lady is entirely *dependent* **on** our help.

9. He is completely *indifferent* **to** what anyone says about him. (= He does not mind at all what anyone says about him.)

10. We will soon *initiate* you **into** the game. (= We will soon teach you the rules of the game.)

11. Bridget is very *sensitive* **to** any criticism. (= Bridget feels keenly any criticism.)

12. The one cat is very *similar* **to** the other.

NEVER LEAVE OUT "ON" IN SENTENCES LIKE THESE.

1. I went there **on** Tuesday.
2. She saw her **on** Friday.
3. "Come **on** Saturday," he said.

16. TROUBLESOME WORDS

1. PASSED.

       passed
(*a*) John ~~past~~ William on the stairs.

       passed
(*b*) The time ~~past~~ quickly.

       passed
(*c*) The full back should not have ~~past~~ the ball to the goalkeeper.

2. PAST.

(a) I walked ~~passed~~ **past** Mr. West's car.

(b) The white horse went ~~passed~~ **past** the winning post first.

(c) The ~~passed~~ **past** week has been a very busy one for me.

(d) "I've been working for the ~~passed~~ **past** hour over there in that desk."

(e) "It's well ~~passed~~ **past** your bedtime—go on, get upstairs!"

3. TO.

(a) "Where do you go **to** school?"

(b) "It's easy **to** do when you know how!"

4. TOO (*use it to make comparisons*).

(a) He is ~~to~~ **too** short to play in goal (compared to the required height).

(b) The boy is ~~to~~ **too** naughty (compared to an ordinarily-behaved boy).

(c) "Don't be ~~to~~ **too** sad," he said (compared to the suitable amount of sadness for the occasion).

too

(*d*) Peggy was in fact ~~to~~ late, although she thought

too

she was ~~to~~ early (compared to the exact time of arrival).

Too

(*e*) ~~To~~ many cooks spoil the broth (compared to the correct number of cooks).

5. TOO (= ALSO, AS WELL).

   (*a*) They, **too**, will come.

   (*b*) "Bring the child **too**, there'll be room in the car."

   (*c*) That dog has a fine head; his legs are excellent, **too**.

6. TWO (1 + 1).

   (*a*) The **two** cats screeched.

   (*b*) "There are only **two** of us—can't you count?"

   (*c*) One and one makes **two**, and **two** and **two** make four.

17. CAPITAL LETTERS

THE FIRST WORD IN A SENTENCE BEGINS WITH A CAPITAL LETTER.

There was a cry. Where had it come from? The old man turned and looked towards the garage.

A CAPITAL LETTER IS USED FOR THE PRONOUN "I."

"Very well, I will go alone."

"No," Mary said, "I will come with you."

WHEN WRITING THE ACTUAL WORDS SOMEONE SAYS, THE FIRST WORD INSIDE THE QUOTATION MARKS BEGINS WITH A CAPITAL LETTER.

Susan said, "Lend me your dictionary, please."

"Certainly," said Linda. "What's happened to yours?"

"I don't know." Susan said, frowning, "It was in my desk before break."

Betty joined them. "You're always losing things, Susan," she said. "Yesterday it was your pen, and to-day it's your dictionary!"

CAPITAL LETTERS ARE USED TO BEGIN THE NAMES OF PARTICULAR PEOPLE AND THEIR TITLES, ANIMALS, COUNTRIES, TOWNS, RIVERS, DAYS OF THE WEEK, MONTHS, INSTITUTIONS, BRANDS, BOOKS, MUSICAL WORKS, PAINTINGS.

Mary Jane Smith; the Queen of England; the Rev. Mr. Johns; Saint Peter; my dog Toby; North America; Huddersfield; Mount Everest; River Colne; Tottenham Court Road; February; Wednesday; August Bank Holiday; Church of England; Royal Academy; Wolverhampton Wanderers; The Margaret Tabor School; Morris Minor car; Nescafé; "The Tale of Two Cities," by Charles Dickens; "Symphony No. 5 in C Minor," by Beethoven; Claude Monet: "Boulevard des Capucines."

THE NAMES OF GOD AND JESUS, AND WORDS WHICH STAND FOR THEM, BEGIN WITH A CAPITAL LETTER.

God; Father; Jehovah; Jesus Christ; the Holy Ghost; "God was merciful, for He sent His Son."

18. APOSTROPHES

AN APOSTROPHE SHOWS WHERE A LETTER OR LETTERS HAVE BEEN LEFT OUT.

1. "It doesn't work," she cried (= does not).

2. "I'm here" (= I am).

3. "You'd like to come too, wouldn't you?" (= you would; would not).

4. "Here's the book," Father called (= here is).

5. "It's raining, and I'll be cold," said Felicity (= it is; I will).

6. "You're first, he's second, and she's third. It's all arranged," the master said (= you are; he is; she is).

7. "Since they're away, who's coming instead?" asked the scoutmaster (= they are; who is).

'S (APOSTROPHE S) ON THE END OF A NOUN MEANS "BELONG-ING TO" OR "LINKED WITH" ONE PERSON OR THING.

1. This is John's overcoat. ('s shows that something *belongs to* John. What? The overcoat. It is a short way of saying "the overcoat of John.")

2. Whose overcoat is this? It is John's (= the overcoat *of* John).

3. Please bring the donkey's saddle (= the saddle *of the* donkey).

4. I am reading Lady Jane Hazlett's memoirs (= the memoirs *of* Lady Jane Hazlett).

5. He has taken somebody else's hat (= the hat *of* somebody else).

6. St. Paul's Cathedral is in London. (The Cathedral does not belong to St. Paul, but it is *linked* with him by being called after him.)

7. The police have caught his son's murderer. (Again, the murderer does not belong to the son, but is *linked with* him.)

8. It was his mother-in-law's birthday (= the birthday *linked with* his mother-in-law).

9. The dog's owner arrived too late to save the animal. (The owner does not belong to the dog, but is *linked with* him.)

10. I enjoy Dickens's novels.

11. This is James's overcoat.

S' (S APOSTROPHE) ON THE END OF A NOUN MEANS "BE-LONGING TO" OR "LINKED WITH" MORE THAN ONE PERSON OR THING.

1. The girls' purses have been stolen (= the purses *of the* girls).

2. Please bring the donkeys' saddles (= the saddles *of the* donkeys).

3. The heroes' swords glitter brightly in the sunlight (= the swords *of the* heroes).

4. The cats' mistress was always overfeeding them (= the mistress *linked with* the cats).

HARO

ADD 's (APOSTROPHE S) TO "MEN," "CHILDREN," "BRETHREN."

1. The men's boots were worn out.

2. He has read all his children's books.

3. The brethren's food was brought to them after they had sat down around the fire.

19. INDEFINITE ARTICLE

USE "AN" BEFORE "A," "E," "I," "O."

1. She ate **an** *a*pple.
2. William asked for **an** *e*gg.
3. I bought **an** *i*ce-cream.
4. Sheila sucked **an** *o*range.

USE "AN" BEFORE "U" AS SOUNDED IN "UP."

1. He has **an** *u*ncle.
2. It was **an** *u*gly sight.
3. He was **an** *u*ndertaker.

USE "A" BEFORE "U" AS SOUNDED IN "JUNE."

1. Have you ever seen **a** *u*nicorn?
2. She strummed **a** *u*kulele.

3. It was **a** *u*nanimous vote.

USE "AN" BEFORE "SILENT H."

1. **An** *h*our passed slowly.
2. He was **an** *h*onest man.

3. The lawyer asked if **an** *h*eir had been found.

20. HYPHENS

WHEN A HYPHEN IS USED TO LINK TWO WORDS TOGETHER,
IT CHANGES THEIR MEANING.

1. He hit the bull's-eye (= the target).
(*Compare:* He hit the bull's eye (= the eye of the bull).)

2. A first-class report was given by the director of the company. (*Compare:* A first class report was given to Mary when she was six.)

3. Six-inch nails were used, the planks were so thick. (*Compare:* Six inch nails were used to fasten the cover to the box, one in each of the corners and two in the middle.)

4. He did a quick calculation and said, "There must be a hundred-and-fifty-odd boots in the store." (*Compare:* The maniac stole only left boots. As a result, there were a hundred-and-fifty odd ones in stock.)

HYPHENS OR NOT?

Writers and dictionaries differ in their use of hyphens. Do we write "head mistress", or "head-mistress," or "headmistress"? What do the dictionaries in your class give?

Obey these two rules:

1. When in doubt, follow a good dictionary.

2. Stick to your decision, at least in the same piece of writing, e.g., if you begin by writing "headmistress," go on writing "headmistress."

RULES FOR MAKING AND USING SENTENCES

THE following rules will help you to correct your common-est mistakes in making and using sentences. A reference to them when necessary will also prevent you from making a mistake.

21. SINGULAR OR PLURAL VERB?

USE "IS," "WAS," "SEES," "WALKS," ETC., AFTER ONE ONLY. USE "ARE," "WERE," "SEE," "WALK," ETC., AFTER MORE THAN ONE.

1. John **is** at school.
   John and Richard **are** at school.
2. He **was** at school with me.
   He and Sheila and I **were** all at school together.
3. The dog **sees** Sheila.
   The dog and cat **see** Sheila.
4. The man with his donkey **walks** away.
   The man and his donkey **walk** away.

Note:
   Bread and butter **is** very nice for tea.

"WAS" OR "WERE"?

was
(*a*) I ~~were~~ in the car.

were
(*b*) You ~~was~~ the only one.

41

were
(c) We ~~was~~ shouting.

were
(d) They ~~was~~ there.

(e) "*Who* **was** there?" "*We* **were** there."

THESE NOUNS OR PRONOUNS REFERRING TO A GROUP ARE FOLLOWED BY A SINGULAR VERB.

1. The *assembly* **is** at nine o'clock every morning.

2. A *herd* of goats **was** browsing on the common.

3. The *flock* of sheep **hurries** towards the farmer's daughter each time she goes to the gate.

4. A *collection* of valuable pictures **was** stolen from the art gallery.

5. *Everyone* } **is** expected to listen.
   Everybody

6. *Anyone* } who **relies** on himself is wise.
   Anybody

42

1. The *people* **are** getting impatient waiting for the concert to begin.

2. *Some* **are** coming, *some* **are** not.

THESE NOUNS OR PRONOUNS REFERRING TO A GROUP ARE FOLLOWED BY EITHER A SINGULAR OR PLURAL VERB.

1. $\begin{cases} \text{The } \textit{audience} \textbf{ listens.} \\ \text{The } \textit{audience} \textbf{ listen.} \end{cases}$

2. $\begin{cases} \text{The } \textit{public} \textbf{ is requested.} \\ \text{The } \textit{public} \textbf{ are requested.} \end{cases}$

3. $\begin{cases} \text{The } \textit{congregation} \textbf{ sings.} \\ \text{The } \textit{congregation} \textbf{ sing.} \end{cases}$

4. $\begin{cases} \text{The } \textit{crowd} \textbf{ has} \text{ all gone.} \\ \text{The } \textit{crowd} \textbf{ have} \text{ all gone.} \end{cases}$

5. $\begin{cases} \textit{None} \text{ of the passengers } \textbf{was} \text{ hurt when the plane crashed.} \\ \textit{None} \text{ of the passengers } \textbf{were} \text{ hurt when the plane crashed.} \end{cases}$

"EITHER . . . OR"? "NEITHER . . . NOR"?

1. *Either* John *or* Mary **is** coming (= one *or* the other *is*).

2. *Neither* John *nor* Mary **is** coming (= *no one is* coming).

3. *Either* the boys *or* the girls **are** coming (= the *boys are* coming *or* the *girls are* coming).

4. *Neither* the boys *nor* the girls **are** coming (= *they are* not coming).

22. TENSE (OR TIME)

NOTE CAREFULLY THE RULE FOR USING TENSES, AND THE EXAMPLES.

You can describe an event as having already taken place in the *past*, or as happening in the *present* whilst you write, or as occurring some time in the *future*. The verbs you use to tell of these events must be in the corresponding tense or time: past, or present, or future.

1. (*a*) He **kicked** the ball.
   (*b*) He **was kicking** the ball.
   (*c*) He **has kicked** the ball.
   (*d*) He **has been kicking** the ball. } *Past*
   (*e*) He **had kicked** the ball.
   (*f*) He **had been kicking** the ball.
   (*g*) He **did kick** the ball.

2. (*a*) He **kicks** the ball.
   (*b*) He **is kicking** the ball.
   (*c*) He **does kick** the ball. } *Present*
   (*d*) The ball **is being kicked**.

3. (*a*) He **will kick** the ball.
   (*b*) He **will be kicking** the ball. } *Future*
   (*c*) He **will have been kicking** the ball.

44

The simple rule is to *keep to the tense you begin with* unless there is some good reason to change it. In the passages for reference below, **bold** words show where the tense is correctly changed, thus:

1. PAST TENSE.

    (*a*) Jack *shouted*. The figure instantly *disappeared*. Jack *moved* cautiously forward. From nowhere, a cobweb *brushed* against his forehead.

    (*b*) The dog *barked* just as Sam, who *had been digging* for only five minutes, *was levering* the box from the loose earth. It *had seen* something. In sudden fright Sam thought "I *have been making* too much noise, I *used to do* better than this, I **am getting** old. In a minute I **shall be caught**, clumsy fool that I **am**."

2. PRESENT TENSE.

    (*a*) The man *whistles*. Instantly the horse *trots* up to him. The man *springs* into the saddle. The horse *rears*, *whirls* round, and *neighs* savagely. Its forefeet *crash* to the ground; the parching dust *spurts* yellow about its hooves.

    (*b*) At last he *sees* a little more clearly and *begins* to walk forward again, but now his steps *are wavering* uncertainly. His thoughts *race* on—he *is being forced* to the conclusion that only one person **had murdered** the old man.

    His lips *move* and a hoarse voice that he *does* not *recognize* as his own *is whispering*: "I **have come** here only to be killed. Why **did** I? I **shall be killed**, I *know* it, unless I *can* get away from here at once."

3. FUTURE TENSE.

    (*a*) "We *shall have* the opportunity of meeting again shortly. Mary *will be coming*. Even more important, you *will be* there. What about David?"

    (*b*) At six o'clock this evening his wife *will be going* to him. By then he *will have been working* for 56 hours non-stop. If his calculations **are** correct, it was the chemical he **told** us about that **caused** the explosion. As she **goes** to take him some food, I *shall be waiting* outside.

TROUBLESOME TENSES.

BECOME.

    (*a*) He **became** a hero yesterday.

    (*b*) She *has* **become** bolder.

BEGIN.

    (*a*) They **began** to sing an hour ago.

    (*b*) You *have* **begun** to grow thinner.

CATCH.

    caught
    (*a*) We ~~catched~~ the fish last week.

    have caught
    (*b*) They ~~catched~~ cold.

COME.

    came
    (*a*) The ball ~~come~~ over the wall just now.

    came
    (*b*) "You ~~come~~ home late the other night, didn't you?"

46

has come
(c) He ~~come~~ home late several times.

"DID" OR "DONE"?

did
(a) I ~~done~~ it.

did
(b) She ~~done~~ the other painting.

did
(c) We ~~done~~ it yesterday.

did
(d) They ~~done~~ it quickly.

did
(e) You ~~done~~ it, I saw you.

did
(f) Who ~~done~~ it?

did
(g) What ~~done~~ the damage?

did
(h) He ~~done~~ the climb.

did
(i) I ~~done~~ the work alone.

did
(j) They ~~done~~ it before we came.

DIG.

dug
(a) Sam ~~digged~~ the garden on Monday.

dug
(b) They ~~digged~~ it over several times.

DRAW.

   (*a*) We **drew** our pay on Friday.
   (*b*) She **had drawn** a huge face.

   (*c*) "What was the result of the football match Sam?"

Sam replied, "We **drewed** 'em."

drew with (correction above "drawed")

EAT.

   (*a*) We **ate** it all two days ago.
   (*b*) *Having* **eaten** it, he was still hungry.
   (*c*) You *had* **eaten** the pie all by yourself.

FLY.

   (*a*) The boy and his father **flew** to Paris at midday.
   (*b*) You *have* **flown** before, surely?

FREEZE.

   (*a*) Donald nearly *froze* to death.
   (*b*) I *was* **frozen**, the water was so cold.
   (*c*) The snow *having* **frozen**, the roads became very treacherous.

GROW.

   grew
   (*a*) They **growed** very tall.

   grown
   (*b*) *Having* **growed** so tall, they had to stoop to get in at the door.

PAY.

    (*a*) We **paid** him last year.

    (*b*) Everyone *had* **paid** him.

RING.

    (*a*) The bell **rang**.

    (*b*) We *have* **rung** the alarm.

RUN.

    (*a*) Peter **ran** fastest of all.

    (*b*) She *has* **run** a good race.

SEE.

    (*a*) He **saw** the robbery.

    (*b*) Mary *had* also **seen** the red car.

"SHOULD" OR "WOULD"?

1. *If determination is meant, use* **would**.
    (*a*) I **would** do it even though I knew it was wrong (= was myself *determined* to).
    (*b*) They **would** go, although they had been warned not to (= were themselves *determined* to).

2. *If "used to" is meant, use* **would**.
    (*a*) Brother and sister **would** go at least once a week to see their invalid mother (= used to).
    (*b*) Fred was my best friend at school. We **would** always go together to the football match on a Saturday (= used to).

3. *If "ought to" is meant, use* **should**.
    (*a*) You really **should** go to see your sick brother (= ought to).
    (*b*) They **should** both go at once if they are to keep their promise (= ought to).

"SHOULD HAVE" OR "WOULD HAVE"?

1. *If "ought to have" is meant, use* **should have**.
    (*a*) I **should have** gone; it was my duty (= ought to have gone).
    (*b*) We **should have** gone when we were asked.

2. *If "intended to" is meant, use* **would have**.
    (*a*) She **would have** gone, but she was too ill (= intended to go).
    (*b*) They **would have** gone, so it was fortunate that we managed to stop them.

SING.

(*a*) The choir **sang** melodiously.
(*b*) When they *had* **sung** their song, they went.

SINK.

(*a*) The steamer **sank** without trace.
(*b*) It *had* **sunk** very rapidly.

STINK.

(*a*) The meat went bad and **stank**.
(*b*) Those stale fish *have* **stunk** the place out.

SWIM.

(*a*) He **swam** a fast crawl.
(*b*) We *have* both **swum** a mile.

WRITE.

(*a*) Phyllis **wrote** a long letter home.
(*b*) John *has* **written** to his mother at last.

23. POSITION OF WORDS

1. "Janet was feeding the goat **in a bathing costume**" *should be* "Janet in a **bathing costume** was feeding the goat."

2. "The girls **at the back of the class** are asked to stand" does not mean the same as "The girls are asked to stand **at the back of the class**."

3. "The deer was shot by the keeper **with an injured leg**" does not mean the same as "The deer **with an injured leg** was shot by the keeper."

4. Running across the road, **she was hit by a car**.

5. **She was hit by the car** going at seventy miles an hour.

PUT "ONLY" IN THE RIGHT POSITION TO MAKE YOUR MEANING CLEAR.

1. **Only** Sarah saw her mother on Saturday (= no one else did).

2. Sarah saw **only** her mother on Saturday (= Sarah saw no one else at all).

3. Sarah saw her mother **only** on Saturday (= and on no other day of the week).

TAKE CARE TO KEEP "TO" AND ITS VERB TOGETHER IN A SENTENCE.

to go quickly.
1. He has ~~to quickly go~~.

to leave hastily.
2. David had ~~to hastily leave~~.

at least to take
3. Tell John ~~to at least take~~ some notice.

to be really
4. The teacher took pains ~~to really be~~ understood.

5. We shall have to ~~very thoroughly~~ look into that **very thoroughly**.

24. NEGATIVES

USE ONLY ONE NEGATIVE IN A SENTENCE.

any.
1. Philip could **not** see ~~none~~.

any
2. "We could**n't** get ~~no~~ water there."

anything."
3. "I did**n't** do ~~nothing~~."

anything."
4. "She does**n't** know ~~nothing~~."

anywhere
5. "They were**n't** going ~~nowhere~~ in particular."

52

Note that you can express the same meaning as follows:

1. Philip *could see* **none**.
2. "We *could get* **no** water there."
3. "I *did* **nothing**."
4. "She *knows* **nothing**."
5. "They *were going* **nowhere** in particular."

AFTER A NEGATIVE, USE "OR" TO EXPRESS A NEGATIVE MEANING.

or
1. He does **not** go to the cinema ~~nor~~ to the theatre.

or
2. Jane can**not** knit ~~nor~~ sew.

or
3. Unfortunately Henry has **not** yet skill ~~nor~~ stamina enough to win a place in the first eleven.

4. He is bottom of the class, **not** because he is really
or
dull ~~nor~~ because he has had bad teaching, but simply because he is bone idle.

AFTER A NEGATIVE, USE "EITHER . . . OR" TO EXPRESS NEGATIVE MEANING.

either   or
1. He did **not** go ~~neither~~ to the cinema ~~nor~~ to the theatre.

either   or
2. Jane can**not** ~~neither~~ knit ~~nor~~ sew.

either   or
3. Unfortunately John has **not** yet ~~neither~~ skill ~~nor~~ stamina enough to win a place in the first eleven.

4. He did**n't** see ne~~ither~~ the ten men n~~or~~ the machine gun.

Note: Another way of expressing the same meaning is as follows:

1. He *went* **neither** to the cinema **nor** to the theatre.

2. Jane *can* **neither** knit **nor** sew.

3. Unfortunately John *has* **neither** skill **nor** stamina enough to win a place in the first eleven.

4. He *saw* **neither** the ten men **nor** the machine gun.

TWO NEGATIVES MAKE A WEAK POSITIVE.

1. Sarah is **not un**happy to be chosen for the race (= Sarah is fairly happy to be chosen for the race, but not completely happy). *Compare:* Sarah is happy to be chosen for the race.

2. I should **not** be **un**willing to do it (= I should be quite willing to do it if necessary).

3. It is **not un***reasonable* to ask him (= It is quite reasonable to ask him).

4. He is **nothing** if **not** confident (= He is perhaps over-confident).

NEVER.

1. I will ne~~ver~~ e~~ver~~ do it again.

54

25. PARAGRAPHS

A PARAGRAPH GROUPS TOGETHER SENTENCES WHICH ARE
CLOSELY CONNECTED.

All these sentences are about his appearance.

His face was brutish and menacing. From tiny eyes, red and restless as a ferret's, he darted suspicious glances everywhere. Only an inch of forehead was visible between his heavy brows and the sweat-soaked hair above. His nose was smashed flat on his face; the grim line of his lips expressed his hatred of all living things.

He moves.

He growled something and started to move towards me. I saw his grip tighten on the club as he began to raise it.

My flight.

Panic-stricken, I turned and fled. Though the brambles ripped my face and hands, I felt no pain. Terror lent me speed, and with each step I knew that I was outdistancing my pursuer. The brightening light ahead of me told me that I was nearing the edge of the wood: a great wave of thankfulness swept over me. In a moment more I was out in the open and running forward.

My fall.

Suddenly I pitched headlong. I tried to scramble up but at once fell back again, my leg twisted uselessly beneath me.

INDEX

	PAGE
"A" or "an"?	39
ADJECTIVES	24, 25
ADVERBS	26–28
Agree to {on, to, with}	29
Anybody	42
Anyone	42
APOSTROPHES	36–38
Assembly	42
Audience	43
Bear	17
Beat, not "won"	18
Become	46
Begin	46
Borrow, not "lend"	18
BRACKETS	8
CAPITAL LETTERS	35, 36
Catch	46
Choose	18
Collection	42
Collective nouns	42, 43
COLON	7
Come	46, 47
COMMA	3, 4
Comment on	31
Communicate with	31
Compare with	29
Comparison of adjectives	24
Confer with	31
Confide {in, to}	30
Congregation	43
Connive at	31

		PAGE
Conscious of	. . . .	32
Consist of	. . . .	30
Contrast with	. . . .	32
Crowd	. . . .	43
DASHES	. . . .	8, 9
Dependent on	. . . . . .	32
"Did" or "done"?	. . . . . .	47
Didn't ought	. . . . . .	22
Differ from	. . . . . .	30
Different from	. . . . . .	30
Dig	. . . .	47
"Done" or "did"?	. . . . . .	47
Draw	. . . .	48
Eat	. . . .	48
Either . . . or	. . . . . .	43
Either . . . or after negatives	. . .	53, 54
Everybody	. . . . . .	42
Everyone	. . . . . .	42
EXCLAMATION MARK	. . . . .	11
Flock	. . . .	42
Fly	. . . .	48
Freeze	. . . .	48
FULL STOP	. . . . . .	1, 2
FUTURE TENSE	. . . . .	44, 46
Gone, not "went"	. . . . .	23
"Got"—use a better word	. . . .	23
Grow	. . . .	48
Have, not "of"	. . . . .	18, 19
"He" or "him"?	. . . . . .	15
Herd	. . . .	42
Hers	. . . .	16
HYPHENS	. . . . . .	40

		PAGE
INDEFINITE ARTICLE	. . . . .	39
Indifferent to	. . . . .	32
Infinitive	. . . . .	52
Initiate into	. . . . .	32
"Is" or "are"?	. . . . .	41
Its	. . . . .	25
It's (= It is)	. . . . .	36
Lay	. . . . .	19, 20
"Lay"—see *lie*	. . . . .	21
"Learn"—see *teach*	. . . . .	22
"Lend"—see *borrow*	. . . . .	18
Let	. . . . .	20
Let loose	. . . . .	20
Lie	. . . . .	21
Lose	. . . . .	21
"Might of"—see *might have*	. . . .	19
"Must of"—see *must have*	. . . .	19
NEGATIVES	. . . . .	52–54
Neither . . . nor	. . . . .	53–54
"No"—see *any*	. . . . .	52
None	. . . . .	43
"None"—see *any*	. . . . .	52
"Nor"—see *or*	. . . . .	53, 54
"Nothing"—see *anything*	. . . .	52, 53
NOUNS	. . . . .	12–14
Nouns referring to a group—singular or plural verb?	. . . . .	42, 43
"Nowhere"—see *anywhere*	. . .	52, 53
"Of"—see *have*	. . . .	18, 19
"Of"—see *off*	. . . . .	27
Off	. . . . .	27
On, with days of week	. . . .	32
Only	. . . . .	51
Ought	. . . . .	22

"Ought to of"—see *ought to have* . . . 19
Ours 16

PARAGRAPHS 55
Passed 32, 33
Past 32, 33
PAST TENSE 44, 45
Pay 49
People 43
POSITION OF WORDS 51, 52
Prefer to 30
PREPOSITIONS 29–32
PRESENT TENSE 44, 45
PRONOUNS 14–16
Public 43

QUESTION MARK 11
Quiet 25
Quite 28
QUOTATION MARKS 9, 10

Ring 49
Run 49

See 49
SEMICOLON 5, 6
Sensitive to 32
Sentences grouped in paragraphs . . . 55
"She" or "her"? 15
"Should" or "would"? 49
"Should have" or "would have"? . . . 50
Sing 50
SINGULAR OR PLURAL VERB? . . . 41–43
Sink 50
Some 43
Stink 50
Swim 50

		PAGE
Teach	. . . .	22
TENSE, OR TIME	. . . . .	44–50
Their	. . . .	25
Theirs	. . . . . .	25
There	. . . . . .	16
TIME (see TENSE)	. . . . .	28
TIME (see TENSE)	. . . . .	44–50
Tired of { by / with }	. . . . . .	31
To	. . . .	33
To and its verb	. . . . .	52
Too	. . . . . .	33, 34
TROUBLESOME ADVERBS	. . . .	27, 28
TROUBLESOME TENSES	. . . .	46–50
TROUBLESOME VERBS	. . . .	17–23
TROUBLESOME WORDS	. . . .	32–34
Two	. . . . . .	34
Usen't to	. . . . . .	22
VERBS	. . . . . .	17–23
Wake	. . . . . .	23
"Was" or "were"?	. . . .	41, 42
Went	. . . . . .	23
"Were"—see *where*	. . . .	28
Where	. . . . . .	28
"Who" or "whom"?	. . . .	16
Who's (= Who is)	. . . .	36
"Who's"—see *whose*	. . . .	36
Whose	. . . . . .	36
"Won"—see *beat*	. . . .	18
"Would" or "should"?	. . . .	49
"Would have" or "should have"?	. .	50
Write	. . . . . .	50
Yours	. . . . . .	16